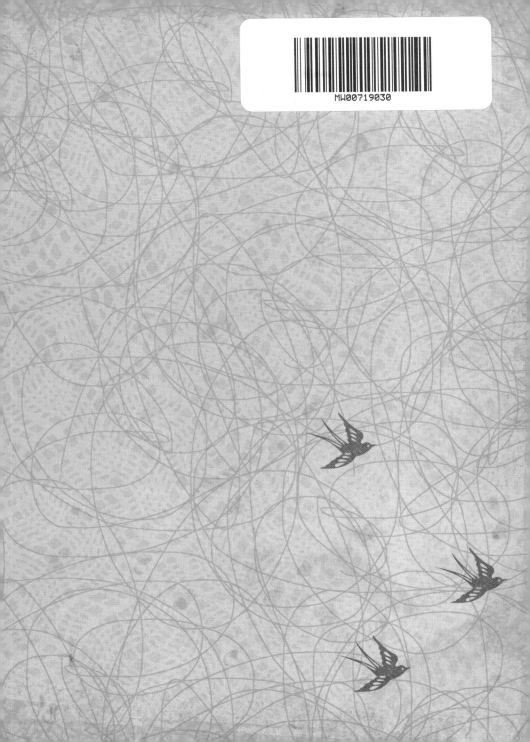

This journal belongs to

Mary fr Betty Jo

You are a beautiful child of God,
precious to Him in every way. As you seek Him,
He will show you the mysteries of life and unfold
His unique plans for you—a life full of rich blessing.

God has given you beautiful dreams to pursue and knows
the desires of your heart. He is as close as breathing. Let this journal
inspire you to express your thoughts, embrace your hopes,
record your prayers, and listen to what God is saying to you.

When dreams come true...there is life and joy.

PROVERBS 13:12 TLB

Dreams

threds

Threds Journals present classic symbols of faith in a fresh
and unexpected way. In addition, each Threds cover shares
a common red thread, a signature symbol of salvation that
Lisa Franke features in her art. The red thread represents the blood of
Christ and the continuing process of transformation
as God weaves His image into our lives.

Ellie Claire
gift & paper expressions

...inspired by life

*G*od created us with an overwhelming desire to soar.... He designed us
to be tremendously productive and "to mount up with wings like eagles,"
realistically dreaming of what He can do with our potential.

CAROL KENT

And so I tell you, keep on asking, and you will receive
what you ask for. Keep on seeking, and you will find.
Keep on knocking, and the door will be opened to you.

LUKE 11:9 NLT

ift up your eyes. Your heavenly Father waits to bless you—
in inconceivable ways to make your life
what you never dreamed it could be.

ANNE ORTLUND

*God can do anything, you know—far more
than you could ever imagine or guess
or request in your wildest dreams!*

EPHESIANS 3:20 MSG

September

Pd $75.00 on Closed Cable acct.

Bal $200.00

Mortgage	560.00
Coventry	46.00
Electric	99.00

*W*herever you go, no matter what the weather,
always bring your own sunshine.

ANTHONY J. D'ANGELO

What matters is not your outer appearance—the styling of your hair, the jewelry you wear, the cut of your clothes—but your inner disposition.

1 PETER 3:3-4 MSG

*ive neither in the past nor in the future,
but let each day's work absorb your entire energies,
and satisfy your widest ambition.

SIR WILLIAM OSLER

*O*h, how sweet the light of day, and how wonderful to live
in the sunshine! Even if you live a long time, don't take
a single day for granted. Take delight in each light-filled hour.

ECCLESIASTES 11:7–8 MSG

When you are inspired by a dream,
God has hit the ball into your court.
Now you have to hit it back with commitment.

ROBERT SCHULLER

But what happens when we live God's way? He brings gifts into our lives...
things like affection for others, exuberance about life, serenity....
We find ourselves involved in loyal commitments.

GALATIANS 5:22–23 MSG

Life begins each morning.... Each morning is the open door to a new world—new vistas, new aims, new tryings.

LEIGH MITCHELL HODGES

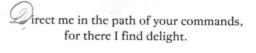

*Direct me in the path of your commands,
for there I find delight.*

PSALM 119:35 NIV

God's gifts put man's best dreams to shame.

ELIZABETH BARRETT BROWNING

How great is the love the Father has lavished on us,
that we should be called children of God!
And that is what we are!

1 JOHN 3:1 NIV

*G*od has designs on our future...and He has designed us
for the future. He has given us something to do
in the future that no one else can do.

RUTH SENTER

I will praise You, for I am fearfully and wonderfully made;
marvelous are Your works, and that my soul knows very well.

PSALM 139:14 NKJV

Shoot for the moon. Even if you miss,
you'll land among the stars.

LES BROWN

Every good action and every perfect gift is from God.
These good gifts come down from the Creator of the sun, moon, and stars,
who does not change like their shifting shadows.

JAMES 1:17 NCV

*Y*our dreams grow holy put into action.

ADELAIDE ANN PROCTER

It's not important who does the planting,
or who does the watering. What's important
is that God makes the seed grow.

1 CORINTHIANS 3:7 NLT

*Though no one can go back and make a brand-new start,
anyone can start from now and make a brand-new ending.*

For I am about to do something new. See, I have already begun!
Do you not see it? I will make a pathway through the wilderness.
I will create rivers in the dry wasteland.

ISAIAH 43:19 NLT

We all mold one another's dreams.
We all hold each other's fragile hopes in our hands.
We all touch others' hearts.

*Encourage one another and build each other up,
just as in fact you are doing.*

1 THESSALONIANS 5:11 NIV

*T*oday is unique! It has never occurred before and it will never be repeated. At midnight it will end, quietly, suddenly, totally.... But the hours between now and then are opportunities with eternal possibilities.

CHARLES R. SWINDOLL

*This is the day the LORD has made;
we will rejoice and be glad in it.*

PSALM 118:24 NKJV

Life is not about discovering our talents;
it is about pushing our talents to the limit
and discovering our genius.

ROBERT BRAULT

*Forgetting the past and looking forward to what lies ahead,
I press on to reach the end of the race and receive the heavenly prize
for which God, through Christ Jesus, is calling us.*

PHILIPPIANS 3:13–14 NLT

The important thing really is not the deed
well done or the medal that you possess,
but the dedication and dreams out of which they grow.

ROBERT H. BENSON

*A*nd now to him who can keep you on your feet,
standing tall in his bright presence, fresh and celebrating—
to our one God, our only Savior, through Jesus Christ.

JUDE 1:24–25 MSG

*G*od is not too great to be
concerned about our smallest wishes.

BASILEA SCHLINK

If God cares so wonderfully for wildflowers that are here today and thrown into the fire tomorrow, he will certainly care for you.

MATTHEW 6:30 NLT

One taper lights a thousand, yet shines as it has shone;
And the humblest light may kindle one brighter than its own.

HEZEKIAH BUTTERWORTH

Let your good deeds shine out for all to see,
so that everyone will praise your heavenly Father.

MATTHEW 5:16 NLT

Go confidently in the direction of your dreams!
Live the life you've imagined.

HENRY DAVID THOREAU

I have come that they may have life,
and that they may have it more abundantly.

JOHN 10:10 NKJV

What we need is not new light, but new sight; not new paths, but new strength to walk in the old ones; not new duties but new wisdom from on high to fulfill those that are plain before us.

The Sovereign LORD is my strength!
He makes me as surefooted as a deer,
able to tread upon the heights.

HABAKKUK 3:19 NLT

Reach high, for stars lie hidden in your soul.
Dream deep, for every dream precedes the goal.

PAMELA VAULL STARR

*The LORD will work out his plans for my life—
for your faithful love, O LORD, endures forever.*

PSALM 138:8 NLT

How wonderful it is that nobody need wait a single moment
before starting to improve the world.

The generous will prosper; those who refresh others
will themselves be refreshed.

PROVERBS 11:25 NLT

*We need time to dream, time to remember,
and time to reach the infinite. Time to be.*

GLADYS TABER

"For I know the plans I have for you," declares the LORD,
"plans to prosper you and not to harm you,
plans to give you hope and a future."

JEREMIAH 29:11 NIV

Be such a person, and live such a life,
that if every one were such as you, and every life a life such as yours,
this earth would be God's paradise.

PHILLIPS BROOKS

God has given us different gifts for doing certain things well....
If your gift is serving others, serve them well. If you are a teacher, teach well.
If your gift is to encourage others, be encouraging.

ROMANS 12:6–8 NLT

*A*mbition is that grit in the soul which creates disenchantment
with the ordinary and puts the dare into dreams.

MAX LUCADO

*P*ursue a righteous life—
a life of wonder, faith, love, steadiness, courtesy.
Run hard and fast in the faith.

1 TIMOTHY 6:11–12 MSG

*B*egin today! No matter how feeble the light,
let it shine as best it may. The world may need
just that quality of light which you have.

HENRY C. BLINN

This service you do not only helps the needs of God's people,
it also brings many more thanks to God. It is a proof of your faith.
Many people will praise God because...you freely share with them.

2 CORINTHIANS 9:12–13 NCV

The stars exist that we might know
how high our dreams can soar.

I pray that you...will have the power to understand
the greatness of Christ's love—how wide and how long and how high
and how deep that love is.... Then you can be filled with the fullness of God.

EPHESIANS 3:18–19 NCV

*The uncertainties of the present always give way
to the enchanted possibilities of the future.*

GELSEY KIRKLAND

*L*ook at those who are honest and good,
for a wonderful future awaits those who love peace.

PSALM 37:37 NLT

*Far away, there in the sunshine, are my highest aspirations.
I may not reach them but I can look up and see their beauty,
believe in them, and try to follow where they lead.*

LOUISA MAY ALCOTT

God hasn't invited us into a disorderly,
unkempt life but into something holy and beautiful—
as beautiful on the inside as the outside.

1 THESSALONIANS 4:7 MSG

See each morning a world made anew, as if it were
the morning of the very first day;...treasure and use it,
as if it were the final hour of the very last day.

FAY HARTZELL ARNOLD

*Teach us to number our days aright,
that we may gain a heart of wisdom.*

PSALM 90:12 NIV

*L*ife...gives you the chance to love
and to work and to play
and to look up at the stars.

HENRY VAN DYKE

*Surprise us with love at daybreak;
then we'll skip and dance all the day long.... And let the loveliness
of our Lord, our God, rest on us, confirming the work that we do.*

PSALM 90:14, 17 MSG

*D*reams are illustrations...
from the book your soul
is writing about you.

MARSHA NORMAN

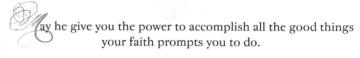

May he give you the power to accomplish all the good things your faith prompts you to do.

2 THESSALONIANS 1:11 NLT

For the human heart is the mirror of the things that are near and far;
Like the wave that reflects in its bosom the flower and the distant star.

ALICE CARY

As a face is reflected in water,
so the heart reflects the real person.

PROVERBS 27:19 NLT

*N*ature decrees that we do not exceed the speed of light.
All other impossibilities are optional.

ROBERT BRAULT

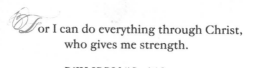

For I can do everything through Christ,
who gives me strength.

PHILIPPIANS 4:13 NLT

Always stay connected to people
and seek out things that bring you joy.
Dream with abandon. Pray confidently.

BARBARA JOHNSON

*H*oney from the honeycomb tastes sweet. In the same way,
wisdom is pleasing to you. If you find it, you have hope for the future,
and your wishes will come true.

PROVERBS 24:13– 14 NCV

What we are is God's gift to us.
What we become is our gift to God.

ELEANOR POWELL

Yes, we should make the most of what God gives,
both the bounty and the capacity to enjoy it, accepting what's given
and delighting in the work. It's God's gift!

ECCLESIASTES 5:19 MSG

At every crossroad, follow your dream.
It is courageous to let your heart lead the way.

THOMAS LELAND

Trust the LORD with all your heart, and lean not
on your own understanding; in all your ways
acknowledge Him, and He shall direct your paths.

PROVERBS 3:5 – 6 NKJV

*E*very person's life is a fairy tale
written by God's fingers.

HANS CHRISTIAN ANDERSEN

*O*n the inside, where God is making new life,
not a day goes by without his unfolding grace.

2 CORINTHIANS 4:16−17 MSG

When we believe in ourselves and never give up,
even our loftiest and most challenging dreams can be realized.

DAVID SAMUELS

I'm not saying that I have this all together, that I have it made.
But I am well on my way, reaching out for Christ,
who has so wondrously reached out for me.

PHILIPPIANS 3:12 MSG

*Those who wish to secure the good of others
have already secured their own.*

A good person gives life to others;
the wise person teaches others how to live.

PROVERBS 11:30 NCV

*Nurture your mind with great thoughts;
to believe in the heroic makes heroes.*

BENJAMIN DISRAELI

You're blessed when you get your inside world—
your mind and heart—put right.
Then you can see God in the outside world.

MATTHEW 5:8 MSG

Christ came to absorb all of life—our family, job, talents, dreams, ministry—into Himself and impress on it His mark.

JEAN FLEMING

Commit your way to the Lord; trust in him and he will do this:
He will make your righteousness shine like the dawn,
the justice of your cause like the noonday sun.

PSALM 37:5– 6 NIV

One way to get the most out of life
is to look upon it as an adventure.

WILLIAM FEATHER

*A*ll God's gifts are right in front of you as you wait expectantly
for our Master Jesus.... God, who got you started in this spiritual adventure,
shares with us the life of his Son.

1 CORINTHIANS 1:7, 9 MSG

It is only with the heart that one can see rightly.
What is essential is invisible to the eye.

ANTOINE DE SAINT-EXUPÉRY

For by him all things were created: things in heaven
and on earth, visible and invisible.... He is before all things,
and in him all things hold together.

COLOSSIANS 1:16-17 NIV

*O*ur truest life is when we are in dreams awake.

HENRY DAVID THOREAU

*A*wake, my soul! Awake, harp and lyre! I will awaken the dawn.
I will praise you, O Lord.... For great is your love, reaching to the heavens;
your faithfulness reaches to the skies.

PSALM 57:8 – 10 NIV

Don't be afraid to take a big step if one is indicated; you can't cross a chasm in two small jumps.

DAVID LLOYD GEORGE

You took a risk trusting me,
and now you're healed and whole.
Live well, live blessed!

LUKE 8:48 MSG

*Hope is not a dream, but a way
of making dreams become reality.*

L. J. SUENENS

The lines of purpose in your lives never grow slack,
tightly tied as they are to your future in heaven, kept taut by hope.

COLOSSIANS 1:5 MSG

You can never change the past. But by the grace of God,
you can win the future. So remember those things which will
help you forward, but forget those things which will only hold you back.

RICHARD C. WOODSOME

*D*o you not know that in a race all the runners run,
but only one gets the prize?
Run in such a way as to get the prize.

1 CORINTHIANS 9:24 NIV

If we all did the things we are capable of doing,
we would literally astound ourselves.

THOMAS EDISON

In all these things we are more than conquerors
through him who loved us.

ROMANS 8:37 NIV

*G*od's touch...lights the world with color
and renews our hearts with life.

JANET L. WEAVER SMITH

You're here to be light, bringing out
the God-colors in the world.... I'm putting you on a light stand.
Now that I've put you there...shine!

MATTHEW 5:14-15 MSG

Give us good dreams and memory of them
so that we may carry their poetry
and mystery into our daily lives.

MICHAEL LEUNIG

How precious to me are your thoughts, O God!
How vast is the sum of them! Were I to count them,
they would outnumber the grains of sand.

PSALM 139:17–18 NIV

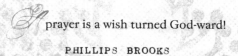
prayer is a wish turned God-ward!

PHILLIPS BROOKS

*Don't worry about anything; instead,
pray about everything. Tell God what you need,
and thank him for all he has done.*

PHILIPPIANS 4:6 NLT

The best and most beautiful things in the world
cannot be seen or even touched.
They must be felt with the heart.

HELEN KELLER

God has made everything beautiful for its own time.
He has planted eternity in the human heart.

ECCLESIASTES 3:11 NLT

*N*ot to dream boldly may turn out
to be simply irresponsible.

GEORGE B. LEONARD

Steep your life in God-reality, God-initiative, God-provisions.
Don't worry about missing out. You'll find all
your everyday human concerns will be met.

MATTHEW 6:33 MSG

*E*verybody can be great...because anybody can serve.
You don't have to have a college degree to serve....
You only need a heart full of grace. A soul generated by love.

MARTIN LUTHER KING JR.

ach one should use whatever gift he has received to serve others,
faithfully administering God's grace in its various forms.

1 PETER 4:10 NIV

*The future belongs to those who believe
in the beauty of their dreams.*

ELEANOR ROOSEVELT

Serving God helps you in every way
by bringing you blessings in this life
and in the future life, too.

1 TIMOTHY 4:8 NCV

*H*ave a purpose in life, and having it,
throw into your work such strength of mind
and muscle as God has given you.

THOMAS CARLYLE

In all the work you are doing, work the best you can. Work as if you were doing it for the Lord, not for people.

COLOSSIANS 3:23 NCV

There are better things ahead
than any we leave behind.

C. S. LEWIS

Let us throw off everything that hinders
and...entangles, and let us run with perseverance
the race marked out for us.

HEBREWS 12:1 NIV

It is necessary that we dream now and then.
No one ever achieved anything from the smallest to the greatest
unless the dream was dreamed first.

LAURA INGALLS WILDER

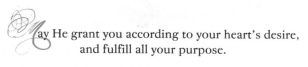

May He grant you according to your heart's desire,
and fulfill all your purpose.

PSALM 20:4 NKJV

Things turn out best for the people
who make the best out of the way things turn out.

ART LINKLETTER

You were taught, with regard to your former way of life, to put off your old self...to be made new in the attitude of your minds.

EPHESIANS 4:22 – 23 NIV

Do not pray for dreams equal to your powers.
Pray for powers equal to your dreams.

ADELAIDE ANN PROCTER

Devote yourselves to prayer with an alert mind and a thankful heart.

COLOSSIANS 4:2 NLT

There is in every human being's heart the love of wonder,
the sweet amazement at the stars and starlike things...the unfailing
childlike appetite for what-next, and the joy of the game of living.

SAMUEL ULLMAN

He will yet fill your mouth with laughter
and your lips with shouts of joy.

JOB 8:21 NLV

God gives us dreams a size too big
so that we can grow into them.

Do not let anyone treat you as if you are unimportant because you are young. Instead, be an example...with your words, your actions, your love, your faith, and your pure life.

1 TIMOTHY 4:12 NCV

Hope is not a granted wish or a favor performed;
no, it is far greater than that. It is a zany, unpredictable dependence
on a God who loves to surprise us out of our socks.

MAX LUCADO

*Dear friend, listen well to my words.... Those who discover these words live, really live; body and soul....
Keep vigilant watch over your heart; that's where life starts.*

PROVERBS 4:20–23 MSG

I look to the future, because that's
where I'm going to spend the rest of my life.

GEORGE BURNS

*Y*our life is a journey you must travel
with a deep consciousness of God.

1 PETER 1:18 MSG

As we grow in our capacities to see and enjoy
the joys that God has placed in our lives, life becomes
a glorious experience of discovering His endless wonders.

Give thanks to the Lord and proclaim his greatness.
Let the whole world know what he has done. Sing to him;
yes, sing his praises. Tell everyone about his wonderful deeds.

PSALM 105:1-2 NLT

Look for the heaven here on earth.
It is all around you.

Truth springs up from the earth,
and righteousness smiles down from heaven.

PSALM 85:11 NLT

Nothing is as real as a dream. The world can change around you, but your dream will not. Responsibilities need not erase it. Duties need not obscure it. Because the dream is within you, no one can take it away.

TOM CLANCY

There is surely a future hope for you,
and your hope will not be cut off.

PROVERBS 23:18 NIV

*G*od's promises are to be the guide
and measure of our desires and expectations.

MATTHEW HENRY

He made the entire human race and made the earth hospitable,
with plenty of time and space for living so we could
seek after God, and...actually *find* him.

ACTS 17:26-27 MSG

....

....

....

....

....

....

....

....

....

....

....

....

....

....

....

....

....

*Pay attention to your dreams—God often speaks
directly to our hearts when we are asleep.*

For God speaks again and again, though people
do not recognize it. He speaks in dreams, in visions of the night,
when deep sleep falls on people as they lie in their beds.

JOB 33:14–15 NLT

This is the true joy in life: the being used
for a purpose recognized by yourself as a mighty one.

GEORGE BERNARD SHAW

You will show me the way of life,
granting me the joy of your presence
and the pleasures of living with you forever.

PSALM 16:11 NLT

*A*llow your dreams a place in your prayers and plans.
God-given dreams can help you move
into the future He is preparing for you.

BARBARA JOHNSON

They delight in the law of the LORD,
meditating on it day and night. They are like trees
planted along the riverbank, bearing fruit each season.

PSALM 1:2-3 NLT

Within each of us, just waiting to blossom,
is the wonderful promise of all we can be.

*Cultivate inner beauty, the gentle,
gracious kind that God delights in.*

1 PETER 3:4 MSG

If one advances confidently in the direction of his dreams,
and endeavors to live the life which he has imagined,
he will meet with a success unexpected in common hours.

HENRY DAVID THOREAU

No eye has seen, no ear has heard,
and no mind has imagined what God
has prepared for those who love him.

1 CORINTHIANS 2:9 NLT

God has a purpose for your life and
no one else can take your place.

We know that all things work together for good
to those who love God, to those who are the called
according to His purpose.

ROMANS 8:28 NKJV

Jesus will give you a peace
that you never imagined was possible...
and a love that perfectly matches your constant wish.

JANET L. WEAVER SMITH

Then you will experience God's peace,
which exceeds anything we can understand. His peace
will guard your hearts and minds as you live in Christ Jesus.

PHILIPPIANS 4:7 NLT

*There is no medicine like hope, no incentive so great,
and no tonic so powerful as expectation
of something better tomorrow.*

May the God of hope fill you with all joy and peace
as you trust in him, so that you may
overflow with hope by the power of the Holy Spirit.

ROMANS 15:13 NIV

*I*t is difficult to say what is impossible,
for the dream of yesterday is the hope of today
and the reality of tomorrow.

ROBERT H. GODDARD

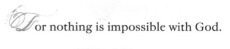

For nothing is impossible with God.

LUKE 1:37 NIV

Ellie Claire™ Gift & Paper Corp.
Minneapolis, MN 55438
www.ellieclaire.com

Dreams

JOURNAL

© 2011 by Ellie Claire Gift & Paper Corp.

ISBN 978-1-60936-164-8

Designed by Lisa & Jeff Franke
Compiled by Barbara Farmer

Printed in China